The Iron City

The Iron City

Poems by

John Bensko

University of Illinois Press

Urbana and Chicago

Library of Congress Cataloging-in-Publication Data
Bensko, John, 1949–
The iron city : poems / by John Bensko.
p. cm.
ISBN 0–252–02554–7 (alk. paper) —
ISBN 0–252–06871–8 (pbk. : alk. paper)
I. Title.
PS3552.E547655I76   2000
811'.54—dc21   99-050618

1 2 3 4 5 C P 5 4 3 2 1

In Memory of John, Julia, Nancy, and Ross

Acknowledgments

The following poems have appeared in the periodicals listed:

"Another Set of Existential Metaphors about the City" and
  "Cinéma Vérité," *The Black Warrior Review*
"Digging It," *The Greensboro Review*
"Winter Scene," *The Iowa Review*
"The Roofer" and "The Window Man," *New Letters*
"Free Delivery," *The Ohio Review*
"The Hidden Street," *Ploughshares*
"Do You Know What High School You Went To?" *Poet Lore*
"The Implied Author," *Poetry*
"Animal Loose along the Parkway," "Plaster of Paris,"
  "Rage for Order," "Rothko," and "Yellow Fever Cemetery,"
  Poetry Northwest
"West Memphis, Southland Track," *River City*
"Mail Bomb" and "The Well," *Solo*

Contents

The Iron City

Part I
The Secrets of Animals

The Iron City

In the big house on Graymont Avenue
the damp coal's smell
cat-and-moused up the cellar stairs
on rainy days, darting on a draft
from under the door.
On the daybed by the rocker
where my father was reading
Josephus's *Wars of the Jews*
I lay still to catch the smells:
first of coal, then his drowsing pipe,
then the kitchen where my mother,
scrubbing down the floor
with a liquid that came and went
sharp as a needle, was whistling
"Old Dan Tucker" like a mockingbird
gone crazy at nesting time.
The high notes rattled my young nerves
like the windows when thunder struck outside.
The song was a family favorite,
played by my grandfather
in his spry courting days
at the banjo-picking barnyard dances.

I was waiting for my father to reach
another passage where I'd seen him before,
his face turning red
as an old prophet's, his bricklayer's
rough hands tightening,
until he'd throw the book
across the room

like a message from God against
the twining wallpaper roses.
It had happened twice.
The book lay, its black cover
torn back, until he'd rouse his pipe
and take a puff, then go over

and dust off the traitorous work.
He was digging after the truth
of the destruction of Jerusalem,
but couldn't sift past the writer's tales
of human treachery.
Josephus, the name sounded like all
the prayers I'd ever heard,
like Joseph and Moses,
Genesis and Judges,
my mind filled with thunder
and the black fires of hell.

Down Graymont and then Third Avenue
to downtown Birmingham,
that was where I'd ride with my mother
on fair-weather days, catching the bus,
sitting up front, but wishing for the thrill
of the wide back seat
where the Negroes rode. They were able to see
everyone, with the whole enormous bus
swaying ahead of them
like a king's royal horses.
I asked my mother why the best seats
were theirs, and she hushed me
with a soft pat on my mouth.

Some things should not be told,
like the future. And some, like the present,
move too quickly. The past is ours
to tell again and again

until it changes as we want it to.
Like Josephus, I look back to the hot
summer days where there was no rain
but the scattering fragments
from the church windows, and the spray
of firehoses on the downtown streets.
I lay on the daybed
and my father fired up his pipe.
Predictability. He rose from the rocker

and lifted Josephus up, like a fat black crow,
dusting him off. My mother's whistling
twined and twirled through the room,
not like a cop's hard, sure whistle
but like a bird's, at nesting time.

The Secrets of Animals

In the sunroom glade of potted plants,
my mother's only pet,
the green parakeet
whose cage in the corner could be
pried opened, would not be still.
It circled and tried
for the windows,
for the pictures on the wall,
anywhere but the cage.

Why can't you be like them, I said.
The seven chalk drawings of animals
between the windows—the hippopotamus,
the alligator—hung still and certain
above their sayings for each day.
Things about tears, about a smile.
The bird's wings were
fan blades. Faster and faster,
they disappeared.

Landing on my shoulder,
the claws were sharp as the fan.
The wings whirled and stilled.
Light as the dust
it smelled like the dust.
Would it like to go outside?
Idling the breeze on trash
behind the shed, the old fan
had not survived my fingers,
now as brazen as soldiers
in their bright slashes of Mercurochrome.

Seven chalk drawings of animals,
but none to say.

My mother shook her head and cried.
She talked of winter coming on,
of the laughter of guests
leaving the party late.
She looked at the animals
on the walls, as if they
and their smiles
had shouldered into the night
the bright disappearing.

Digging It

Birmingham, 1955

Traffic from the avenue hums distant
as my mother's radio in the kitchen window
where she irons the ill-fitting
navy jumpsuits my father slumps into
for the mines. In the terraced garden
behind the house, iris centipede
the rocky ledges. The waspy fallen
figs have abandoned their fragile limbs.
Fossil limestone chunks beg breaking open
to spill the crenelated
fans of wavering seas. Too old
even for dinosaurs, my father said.
Hand over hand, I scrape the dirt.
My friend Michael, older by two years,
and left like me by day to wander,
plunges the pitchfork down.

Where are we going? Anywhere untested,
through the mines my father curses in,
through floors of forgotten seas,
through earth's core, the fiery hell
we measure with a yellow tape stolen
from my mother's sewing basket.
Dirt, and more dirt. Past the roots of iris,
fig, and a long dead oak,
to the dark, the damp, the cool.
Past all sense, until my friend, dazed
above me by the sun, or bored
with watching the flash of my fingers,

jabs the pitchfork down fast
beside me. There isn't time
for the flinch to save my hand.

He pulls up, looks with me at the clean
shine of the metal, at the back
of my hand, like an insect where it lies
as if the red hole has pinned it.
Pain? No, there isn't any.
Free of tears, suddenly older,
I swell in my bravery, slamming
the screen door, striding through the kitchen
for a Band-Aid. My mother takes the hand.
Grandparents close in.
They turn me over and over,
sifting. Their shock
glides cool as wind across my face.
The red hole is all the way through,
deeper than I'd ever hoped.

The Priest at the Mine

The last chamber opens empty, and your wife,
falling to her knees, is forced out
from hope. I watch the men carry her
down the hill. The pump slows to a stop,
the earth fills. Men, like trapped
insects, press their shapes into coal.
I see more clearly now. You, deep
in a dark pocket, are all of us
who breathe toward extinction.

What good is celebration? Prayers
at best are music. Let us say, we remember
the fine work in the church. The two
lovely children. The garden where
the roses you pruned were the colors
of the rainbow. Closer than you
should these instead be dug up?

On the hill behind our house, where gullies
cut deep into the yellow shale,
I see you and I, as boys, digging there,
pulling out the textured pieces
of fossilized trees, carting them
down to show the family. Then,
our great aunts whispered.
It was the work of devils.
Mother made us bury the pieces.

Is the man with the pipe a part of you?
I was eleven, you twelve, a spring night.
Walking onto the porch after dinner, I saw

him sitting on the rock wall beside the church.
He held a pipe in one hand, the smoke curling
slowly above his head. Down the road,
the corner lamp was buzzing and I watched
the moths circle in. There was a smell in the air
of burning tobacco, and the smell grew odd
when you showed me the man's shadow
angled toward the light.

The mine is a shadow,
the smell of coal like nothing else.
Wet, it enters your very heart, the oil
of damp earth rock you know on a winter morning
will burn low and blue
to warm the room. Here in Brookside,
where our grandfathers came
hiding the old country behind them
with their worn-out boots in a sack,
because one day they might need
to put them back on, like the Apostles
speaking in the Spirit,
everyone spoke coal.

Coal is life, death. Can it be
so simple? The mine is a shadow.
It reaches into daylight.
There are no rocks to roll back,
only the terrible crush of shadow.

Down the hill is Five Mile Creek,
and the swinging footbridge across to town
where we played, tossing down paper gliders
to float on the water.
They'll be taking your wife across there
to the house. The two girls will be waiting.
It would keep me safe if I could stop
wondering, as we all do

how it has happened.
The rock around us has tightened its air.
We are still breathing, listening
for the tap of a hammer.

The Missing Foot

When my grandfather had his foot cut off
its absence spoke, simply
but with the resonance

of a prophet: *Make way,* it said,
the path is narrow.
Very old, he had no patience

with the foot. He had less
with its absence. Still
the missing foot would call: *Make way.*

He believes the foot is wandering
up hills behind his house,
to coal mines abandoned since his youth,

the one where his uncle died
and the one where he himself
was buried two days

while rescuers dug him out. *Make way*
through the dripping rock,
through the black dust

and crumbled beams.
The foot hears
the voices and the clangs

of picks and shovels,
so many years in the past
but rescued now, as it makes its way

further up through pines
into the hardwoods
where in spring he hunted

with his father for mushrooms,
white nubs in the leaves,
and the yellow shelves

along damp trunks
fallen to the ground,
and the brown trumpets

with their silent call.
For this, he hates the foot
and he hates its absence. *Make way.*

After his father died,
he went to the graveyard
unable to sleep, and lay

on the damp soil of the grave
spilling the tears
of a hundred whippings

and a hundred forgivings
until a tree moved
toward him. *Make way.*

Tree and foot,
are they together? Out there
waiting for him?

He can't hear.
He can barely walk. *Make way,*
the foot says, and the tree

bends toward him with its
whips and smiles. *The path
is narrow. Make way.*

Rage for Order

For my grandfather Blanton, over six foot six
and able to see a country mile,
the garden rows were never straight enough,
fixed by transit to his hair's-width

distinctions. To my grandmother, small, wandering
her tight yet nimble fingers
down the lines of beans, nothing mattered
but space enough to put her knees.

He was a mason, the kind that sets up lines
to lay the brick of houses.
All across the county, he'd put up
the walls of churches, sure to last

for centuries. She was his failure,
too small and sure framed
to need the brick at all,
hampered by his weighty visions.

She told him the straighter rows
shone like a beacon for birds.
He answered that birds were not his concern.
Let them fall where they may.

I loved them both, in summers lying
between the rows of iris
they'd transplanted from their city home,
here to the country where stripped

from their terraces the flowers drooped
and shifted their heads, bewildered
as a crew of landlocked sailors

on a wide prairie. Above me
the bees and hummingbirds

wove a sound I thought of
as the cloth of flowers.
While beyond, the two bickering voices

sharpened themselves on each other
like blades of scissors.
I knew enough to stay out
of their endless travels

back and forth from hatred to delight.
Tall, white haired, like a god,
he moved across the new plowed ground
unballing his twine. Already springing up,

and sure to reach his height
sooner than I could hope, I waited
low down, head hidden between the flowers,
knowing she was there somewhere

with me, her small fingers
working the loose earth,
tiny, sure-footed animal
ready to battle him, hair by hair.

The Old Stanton Place

The greenhouses were newspapers
with the words shot out, the story
of a war of glass we'd finished long ago.

After them the barn where the man
who'd bought the place stored his hay,
bale on bale, twenty feet deep,

drifted through summer
with its unsettled dust
as we crawled toward

the discovered, soon-abandoned lairs,
a nest of baby rats, a possum playing dead.
We were still young enough

to notice life, and death, and moving on
without caring about them. And why
the rich man let the old place fall

meant as much as birds we shot
and left for the barn's lurking
pregnant cat we named Louise.

We were from the new development.
No one knew who Stanton was,
a name, a story the greenhouses

wouldn't tell, and the field
with its neat rows of holes
where the plants, whatever kind,

had been dug and carted to wherever
Stanton went. We hated the rich man.
He wanted us off his place,

sending his man on a tractor
to yell police at our speeding backs
as we trailed hay toward the woods

like uprooted trees heading home.
We, like Stanton, knew the place was his,
and thereby ours. Bobby Randolph

was the first to go, moving
to Dallas where his father worked
for an airline. Then the Finolo brothers,

whirled off by divorce to be with their mother
in the paradise of Florida.
School, girls, it's all a story

too easily known. But Stanton
had no story and he was ours,
his place of bulldozed brick

and pans left in the dirt,
all the things out back
to be shot and picked clean,

some kid coming along
finishing them off.

What the Children Saw and Heard

Never leave a house through any other door
than the one you enter.

They're dark and clannish as nuns, the ladies
of the sodality. They lift their dresses
all at once, crossing the muddy slag
to and from Aunt Jaye's back door.

Blinds left up at night will bring
the whirling wind.

When souvenirs from Florida
are seen on the dining table
(too much like an altar) even the delicate
whorls of an ocean are swept away.

A whisper before children
of the pain of birth is ruin.

Aunt Jaye mumbles prayers
to untangle her misguided steps.
She calls us all her hopeless ones.
We watch the dark dresses walk away.

Knives and spoons
must never cross.

She tells us how easy it is
to forget a toe, then a foot,
going out the wrong door.
We're afraid, stepping wild.

Bright shells, we tumble past heaven.

Independent Miner

Dead now, gone back into the hill
where you dug for coal far deeper
than where you lie, you've left behind
the same sloping hillside of yellow crumbly shale,
and above, the pines whose green comes clear in winter
from brush and scrub oak, and the dog's sharp bark
which echoes from the shacks
lining the creek. We stand beside your grave
as mourners. It's hard to think of ourselves
being up here, where the light goes on.

Then, the light came with you
in the brass carbide lamp, its pop of flame
as your thumb rolled steel over flint.
You clipped it to your helmet
and walked into the shaft, pushing
before you the cart, emptied of its coal
the evening before, and now filled with timbers
for shoring, down the seam's drift
of played out coal through the layers
of cap rock to the deeper veins, the new work.

There at the end, you told me once,
and I didn't know whether to believe,
where the night before
you'd shot the charge to loosen the next day's
haul, you found the opening
to the older shaft from another mine
and there the picks and timbers and lamps,
the iron rails of the cart track,
and the two dead men trapped,

preserved in the sealed air
from a rock fall. No one knew
who they were or when they'd disappeared.
Their clothes were from years
before the turn of the century.

I try to imagine you with them now,
preserved, still alive. But then
where would you be? Trapped,
digging the endless tunnels,
every day more of you, more of us
coming to join you?

It was then your story turned
from belief to disbelief. How the next day
you returned to the opened chamber
to retrieve the old tools and timbers.
They'd crumbled to dust. Not only the wood
but the metal, the steel and iron
lying in ghostly shapes of rust.

Maybe it was true, some alchemy
of carbon and pyrite, of air
breathed down by dying lungs
and held for years, until suddenly
the mouth is opened. The fresh life
breathes the held death to dust.
Or maybe it was just an old miner's tale,
meant to tell a grandson
that in a world of rock hard work
where the water drips the time
through a day you never see,
the imagination finds its way.

Abandoned Mine

Up the road to Mount Olive
a place of crickets, the drip of water

so gentle it would put us to sleep.
We needed no warning,

you'd been in the family too long.
Down the trail grown in pines,

our feet on twigs
were sudden as your timbers

unframing themselves. Your mouth
crumbled. Your depths offered

the silence of our grandfathers. No one
wanted in. None dreamed of working down

through rock to foot-thick veins.
Without warning

we pointed you out to those who asked,
the foolish, the fearless, the stranger,

an unwelcome cousin or two.
Standing in the cool air

that rushed from you, we waited
as their voices grew indistinguishable.

Their footsteps clattered down.
From the fall of rock

we needed no warning, gave none.

Late Shift

After midnight, miners like my father
Walked home, steel hats cocked on their heads

As though their work were play. From my window
I waited to see under the streetlamp their faces

Blackened. Except the eyes.
The whites blazed through.

Coal, the rock that burns. Memory of delicate
Ferns, leaves, bones of fishes

Breaking forth. Build a fire to warm a house,
In a furnace force the air, until ore gives up

Its pure, molten steel.
The oily smudges across my fingers

From filling the bucket in the shed
I pressed on white paper. The prints

Were mine alone, my father said.
I threw them in the fire and watched them curl.

Coal burning gives a smell that fills
Each breath. Its sweetness comes late

To the tongue. Its faint smoke
Over time touches the streets, the yards,

And finds itself gathering
Even within the walls of the house.

Brookside, Alabama

Long after most films went to color
they were still without sound
in the Brookside theater.
The grainy black and whites were matched
by the owner's daughter at the piano
pounding out the chase, or lilting through
gentle cascades of love.

Even the people had voices far
from the drawls of downtown
Birmingham, only twenty miles away.
Weekends, I'd ride with my parents
to my father's family
down the deadman curves
of Cat Mountain and along Five Mile Creek
which, as far as I could tell,
ran forever. Past the barren shale
of strip mines, and the clear
acid water pits, we'd come to a valley
where the sulfurous water of the treatment plant
announced slag-covered streets
of unpainted high porches, where
the eyes of men and women
stared deeper than the mines.
They still kept to dark clothes from the old country
as proudly as their language I didn't know.

Once, with my grandfather in the silence
of the Russian church, I gazed at smoke
glazed icons of the grim yet passive saints

and whispered: What is heaven?
Nothing we know, he said.
It's where the dead live.

In Brookside, they walked the streets,
or so my father swore,
having seen himself the woman
nine feet tall who guarded the footbridge,
and the man whose coffin would not allow itself
to be carried into church.

Like the coal mines, they're
played out now, all they
whose language was wrong, who stalked
street and porch in black and white
past their time and place.
They're silent stars, piano gone,
claimed by color and sound.

Part 2
The Hidden Street

The Ornamental Iron Works and Museum

In the backyard shed, the students
work and sweat the iron stars of David.

The stars hiss, steaming from the bath,
held by tongs, by smeared arms

which offer their singed hairs again
to the bed of coals. Ornaments, badges,

rings, and spikes. Even rows of corn
can turn to iron.

Before it was a museum, it was a hospital,
and before that, a field surrounded

by Confederate earthworks
built on the burial mounds of Indians.

Twain called the bluff
the most beautiful on the Mississippi

where the river comes down from the north
and barges slow

past the city of Memphis,
where they make the strong turn west

boiling up waves
on the wide Arkansas sandbars

of a Spanish land grant
before turning again south.

A president's daughter
was almost married here.

Send a man into frontline battle
with no more than this:

a pole tipped by a *fleur de lis.*
Having learned perhaps from God

beauty is destiny
when ornament is iron,

David took Bathsheba
and kept his star alive.

The students, finishing their stars,
line them in a row. Seven stars

to fill a fence, or top a gate.
There's no history here,

no reckoning for what one
or the other might do,

except the lesson of heat.
Jack, the man who teaches,

jerks his blunt thumb up to tell
them all: the hotter the fire,

the quicker the turn.
On the sill of the workshop

a stray cat takes its rest
licking its long furred paws

above a row of blackened heads of ducks,
while the curved stems of a banister

climb to nowhere, and the roostered
vane sleeps across the floor.

Owning a House

The dogs are barking and the women
from the retirement condo
are rushing through the parking lot
with bags of groceries
and plans for phone calls
saying *Dogs, dogs, dogs,*
and then total silence.

The dogs are barking and the lights
come on in the penthouse,
sleepless penthouse with its
flowering plants on the veranda
and its secret knowledge of black
vans circling the block
in search of someone, anyone, you.

The dogs are barking, barking,
and the mockingbird is chattering
and the rain and wind
are rattling the tin cans
left on the driveway. For sale
signs are going up of their own
accord. The houses built

on clay, on sand, rise up,
look over at each other,
how close they are,
and while the dogs are barking
they move, just a little
at first, but then more
and more and more.

You have built your house
where the dogs are barking
and only prayer will keep it in place,
prayer and storm windows.
Put a window on top of a window,
use ear plugs, call a lawyer,
the health department,

the coroner. The dogs are barking
and they will dig you up
from your sleep, the deep sleep
of the damned. Aren't you glad
you bought this place?
There's room for a garden
in the backyard, and maybe

a fountain, with a few stones.
You can plant your way out of this,
you're sure. It's not your time.
Clever perennial, you'll slip off,
then resurrect. Even if the dogs
are barking, that's not why
the bricks are cracking, the roof

is leaking, the ground is
settling. You're sure. Absolutely
sure, now that you have
the papers and you're making
the payments, that you did
the right thing. Let them bark.
You own this place.

Free Delivery

Begin bare floored

with extra large supreme
bringing its incense of sweet peppers
and cheese like an overgenerous uncle
who's the life of Christmas
the first two kisses he's there.

Then, a chair, its arms scrolled
and gilded, perhaps not the throne
of a king, but at least the favorite
of the youngest prince, hand on chin, plotting
the eternity of his brothers.

A rug rolls in, the red carpet
announcing its dignitary, you,
not quite sure it's in
the right place, or if it likes
your scuffing bare-footed across it.

Your love, late, sweetly late,
sweeps in and settles across from you.
Open her doors. Watch her
in darkness, how she lights the room.
She's music. Never leave her alone.

Finally, the flowers, did I say
flowers of the grave, the wreath
for stones and doors? No, not yet. Flowers
of marriage, flowers of moving in.
Flowers of success and anniversary.

What's left out?
Babies, yes, these days. And no more
the kindly stethoscope, leaning
over your bed. Still, the end,
the end will always come

freely, padding down the hallway
on its softening feet.
Out in the van your wishes plead,
address wrong . . . number lost . . .
at the hapless driver racing the night:

Flowers, more flowers, please!

Another Set of Existential Metaphors about the City

Always they were waiting, like a set of fingers
on top of the lunch counter, occasionally
tapping in anticipation of the waitress's
arrival. What is the point in such comparisons,
in such arrivals at only partly-significant
connections? The point to avoid
is the concrete conclusion, until one's anticipation
of it becomes so abstract that it steps in
like the waitress: she arrives suddenly,
a hand on her hip in the eloquence of one's daydream
to announce there is no more pie.

Yes, just another existential metaphor
for the city. Its fragments of experience
catch up with him in the strangest places,
like the tie he wore only once. It falls
from his coat pocket in the subway
to remind him of the night he tried
to pick up the waitress. The other patrons
drum their fingers on the counter top.
You can see the story coming together.
It is like something your grandfather
told you one day which made no sense.
The next day, another detail fell out,
and then he finally twisted the whole herring-bone
of events into a day that happened to him
when he was a young man. In the same way, memory
postpones connections. As if it's an old man playing

a game on you, it keeps things interesting.
The names of starlets, of towns you were almost
forgiven in, lie on the tip of your walk
into the cafe where the waitress says:
Butt out! I don't like your tie.
In the real world

which is to say the one where people die,
the existential metaphor for the city
is just another joke. The waitress smiles.
The tie is you! The only problem is
you have never been born.

This is why many of us avoid the city.
We lie in the fields, chewing blades of grass,
like cows or something else. We know enough
to avoid the love of urban things.
The misery we live in
is the fact that our houses, our lands, the woods
where we walk, and the streams
where we soak our feet and watch leaves
slowly drift by, are merely the more cunning
metaphors for the city. The old man, leaning over the fence,
is just one more pastoral existentialist.
The city in his head contains all
the waitresses for whom men will die.
Hi ya neighbor, he says. He plays out the best
accent the rural scene can bless. The illusion,
God we love it, is that he *is* our neighbor,
that he *is* and *always has been*
from the country—isn't that like

the guy next to you at the lunch counter?
He says: *Hi ya neighbor.* He leans over the fence.
While you cool your feet a little longer,
the waitress hustles by you, like leaves.

Trailer

Lover of floods,
Tornado magnet, unreliable coffin,
Once, my car broken down,
I learned to live in one

In Florida where every day
That time of year
Clouds darkened the west,
Guy wires outside hummed,

The floor shook,
The wind lifted the sharp
Edges of the roof.
It belonged to the father

Of an Iroquois chief, back north
For the summer,
Whose picture of some New York
Cardinal, looming behind

The dining table
With pressed hands, froze the need
To be prayed over constantly.
In my sleep, the plastic

Mary finger bowl of holy water
Hanging by the bed
Was a lake. All the trailers
Were Cortés's soon-to-be-conquered

Pagan city of the Mexica
Floating on its thousand singing islands.

The neighbors weren't so bad,
Most too old

Even to be cranky.
Trailers, some people say
You've got to be crazy
Or trash or both

To live in one.
I grew to accept
The slow scraping roll
Of walkers moving to the mail boxes.

The ambulances
Hushed down the lanes
Like casual cats. Their doors
Clicked softly shut.

The only commotion:
Familiar thunder in the west,
The whirling cloud
Up to heaven,

The cry of the occasional dog
Disappearing by the pond
Into the mouth of the alligator
Older than us all.

The Roofer

In the end, the world will sound like me:
A half-crazed man in scorching heat
Banging a hammer on your roof.

The ones I like: old ones,
Shingled three or four thick,
The last layer curling black,

The whole roof caving.
Flat-bladed shovel in hand
I scrape the rubble off, drive down nails,

Patch the rotted wood.
And if I miss my work?
Remember the peace of collapsed

Country shacks? The scent
Of purple trumpet flowers? Go on,
Deny the roof makes the house

More than the house makes the roof.
Soon, my footsteps will be gone.
My scraps in the yard

Will wait like leaves.
Listen carefully.
It's my favorite joke, you know,

To stand above and gaze
To the waves of heat rising
From distant rooftops . . .

Then to leave my mark,
One crack
To keep me coming back.

West Memphis, Southland Track

Drive past the section the locals call
little Vietnam, where even the city appraiser
won't go without a bodyguard,
cruising through with note pad
and cautious eye, so the gutted
and the lived-in he values
by the same exterior gaze—

out past the Blue Beacon truck stop
where in the evening the orange
of sodium vapor lights the sleepy hookers
sidling the lanes to their Citizens Band
directions, and truckers doze in their rigs
after the long haul across Texas,
Oklahoma, Arkansas—

but not as far as the cotton fields
where firework stands sprout from derelict
chicken houses decorated by artists
of the explosive husbandry of fowl
with the flare of rockets along whitewashed sides—

and certainly not
as far as the looted Indian mounds
and the abandoned gin, a Stonehenge
of concrete pillars where teenagers have marked
in the blood of German Shepherds
and, some say, of children,
their Satanic signs

turn instead a mile inside the levee
by last year's track of the killer tornado
that flattened a half dozen liquor stores
to the Southland lot, where the gamblers
and their sure-fire greyhounds
were that night saved—

then, walking, pass the tipsters
whose red and blue and yellow sheets
wave you to the winner's circle,
their names a military code—
Trackman, Double Key, Red Dog—
find a spot by the rail where the sleek,
starved animals come in, while the bettors
with comb and paper, buzz each to mark
the turn of eye and twitch of tail—

Southland,
with the enormous woman in blue
immeasurably friendly, talking to herself
of linens and lamps and men who have
betrayed her, who reaches down her dress
to retrieve from the crease between
her breasts her crumpled, sweaty bills—
Ladies and Gentlemen, place your bets.

The Hidden Street

The dogs have stopped barking. Even the grass
has grown quieter, holding back from the wind.
As you and I walk down the sidewalk, our voices
are like a memory, whose deep
purpose has gone inside, into the walls
and floors and ceilings, where it no longer
reaches the air but lies in wait for us.

Where did we take the wrong turn? Some might
say it was right, onto this street
of Victorian houses, with their cupolas
of children looking down, and owners
sweeping their wide porches, as if the dust
they raise were sound, and the faces
pressed against glass were not boredom

but the shouts of afternoon games.
Have you and I become hawks
sweeping forceful pinions above
the dim unsuspecting? Or are we moths
attracted to windows, while preferring
the dark corner and the night?
The street has no answer. Its voice

is victim, is night. It is the hidden
street we walk down afternoons
surprised to find it once more, to recognize
its antique beauty, its deadly silence.

The Well

As in the old country, they dug them
wide enough to climb into.

But the man with pick and shovel,
who took the ground from under himself,

was not there, where I helped my mother
pull off the boards that saved from falling in

dogs, children, the nightroaming
drunks. We stared down

to the cast of light upon the trash
that grew a scurry of rats

where once the digger stood.
He must have lowered himself,

foot, then knee, then waist.
Grass at his eyes, he went under

until the sky receded
to a circle of blue.

Heaven no more
than the span of thumb wrapped

to forefinger, a little O.
Then, the water seeping in.

How did he get out? I asked her.
My mother, imagining no more

than what we saw, tossed in
the day's trash, and said, *Who?*

I don't know, I said.
In Brookside, the wells went bad

house by house. Their stones were pulled down,
their bottoms filled. Except the one

old man Chervinsky kept, neat with flowers
around its sides. The roof of cedar shingles

held straight. The bucket was ready
for the pulley's creak and swing.

He showed me how the well
stayed cool on blazing days.

He turned the wooden crank
and tipped the water toward me,

undrinkable mirror reflecting the sky
and my fingers dipping in.

Night Tennis

After one, on a warm night, my windows open,
I hear the *tock, tock* from the neighbor's yard
but all is dark. They are

the original owners, the rest of us small,
suburban. They're still of the country
where their grandfather raised

prize quarter horses, the land around them
tightening like the turn of such a horse
quicker than you can imagine.

By day, they are friendly, waving through
the wrought iron fence
where brick gives way to gate

as if guarded by the aimless
gardener who kneels in the beds
or moves a hose from lawn to lawn.

The horses are gone, replaced by a pool
and the court, where now they play
deep in the night, no moon, no lights.

Tock, tock, and the huffing breath,
the slap and squeak of shoes.
Why no lights, I wonder, and I go

to the window, barely able
to make them out, past the row
of cedars along the fence

the two of them in whites
dancing at a distance
across the dark rectangle.

No sign of a ball, no sign of rackets.
Tock, tock. They can't
be making it up, moving

so frantically in the dark.
Wild bees tied by a string
we are possessed by each other.

Animal Loose along the Parkway

Unlike you, they know I'm up here,
those men with nets
surrounding the trees
this side of the zoo.

You drive by, late from work.
Like the evening air
rushing past your arms
I'm your fear

of putting the Memphis skyline
behind you. Down Pigeon Roost Road
lie a dozen sweet miles
of Mississippi mud

called Dead Man's Slough.
The zoo men are certain.
They look in the limbs
after something of theirs

which has climbed to a safety
they can never allow.
Tiger, snake? You have no clue.
How often have you

carried the net?
Your hand wavers on the shift.
They fed me well, you think.
They gave me their smiles

and the laughter of their children.
Let the street sounds
escape. Creep higher.
We are unretracted like a claw.

Part 3
The Victims of Love

The Implied Author

He could be anyone,
but more importantly, he is not. . . .
—Marcel Proust

More important than the trees
is their connection with the lake
on which my father rowed
that afternoon, while the swans
were being chased by my sister
back and forth along the bank.
In the new dress which she'd worn
only once, because it was
her Easter dress, white with yellow lace
at the cuffs, she was now
the object of my desire, now the focus
for what would, after long work, become
my masterpiece. I will never
appear there, I thought.

I thought of myself, the shy
one who marked the angles
between the trees, their shadows
on the lake, and the hidden sun's
implied face, striking at their surfaces.
Where was I in all this bother?
Where the girl and her boyfriend
teased each other with threats
along the slippery bank?
Where my father drifted, now
having put down the oars and rested
his head on the stern of the boat

to look into the clouds, to fall
asleep? Nowhere, and yet the implication
of the sun was that it was
behind the trees, cutting an angle
of light and dark gold across
the straw of my father's tilted hat.

I was almost painterly
in my need for supposition,
for suggestions which create
the pictures of myself
which have no limits.
In the art of distant,
almost unreachable emotions
I found the clue which no one
who guesses for allusions can have missed:
the feather lying in the grass, half-concealed
where it dropped from the tail of a swan.
A small, white reminder,
it could mean almost anything. It can
mean a slip of the hand, a word
from the lips which become
the lips of a girl, a lover,
an obsession with that day
which no longer holds meaning.
At least, I like to tell myself
it holds no meaning.
All this trickery, you think, and then . . .

the inescapable evidence
lies there: the delicate spine
of the feather in the palm
of my character's hand. Like me
he daydreams past the abstract world
of symbol, until the feather
becomes the physical evidence
of his inability to touch anyone.

Like the author
of a detective story
who wakes to find he has never written a word,
only acted it out,
I must become the guilty one . . .
Only then is it possible
for the others, my friends,
relatives, the townspeople who knew
me as a boy, to reach the necessary
contradiction, to say: No,
it is not him. They shake their heads
knowingly at my love for confession
and they say: Yes. It was the other . . .

who killed the father, who turned
the sister into the mother
of his child. And if one like me,
so caught up in the trickery of his own
innocence, creates the story
of his guilt, they understand.
When they read my confession of that day
by the lake, breathe as my character did
once more the spring air, and hear the wings
of the frightened swans, the fact

that it happens now as it happened
then is all the illusion
they need: He is one of us.
This strange story of their refusal
to see him as anything less
than what they create
is what I find for my answer:

I appear, suddenly whole,
stepping from behind the trees.
The artist is not merely the feet moving quickly
across the grass toward the feather,

not merely the hand reaching down.
The boat drifting across the lake
belongs to his father.
His sister calls. He will show them
something more than a symbol,
his discovery: how a feather
held in the hand of his character
and turned in the sunlight
will absorb their attentions
until he disappears.

Do You Know What High School You Went To?

On the bus north of Laredo the border man stops
and eyes the kid beside me, both
wearing sunglasses, although the kid's
are not as dark. "Where you from," the man says.
And the kid, cheerful, "Laredo, man."

The border man's glasses rise on his face
as if behind them ice has floated to the surface.
"What high school did you go to?"
We watch them step into the air-conditioned trailer,
where someone removes the kid's cap and shades.

Has anyone, anywhere, ever looked so foreign?
The border man comes back, no dark glasses,
but pale blue eyes and a warm smile at the driver.
"We'll be keeping this one."
Like a catch he's measured beyond the limit

of high school, home street, name
of the corner store where the guys hung out
calling to the girls. How well do I remember
that corner of my life?
Night traps the familiar voices around me,

unnamed streets,
a border of unnamed stars.

The Window Man

Not quick but green
in my uniform, the slow
ivy clatter and clank
of ladder and bucket,
I climb her office wall
insignia stenciled
over my heart: Summer Inc.

Ancient smiling ritual
of a day when one appeared
at a loved one's door
to give a hand to cleaning,
in the time of glass
I am kept outside
to do my climbing.

I look in, pretending
not to see, knowing
that my foreign eyes to her
have no depth, that my hands
waving the pantomime
of greeting are no more
than the vine's heart-shaped leaf.

To a window so clean
what can I do?
I work patiently
as a rainmaker turns
under an empty sky.
Until I am lost, the lover
she would know of herself

if only she looked for more
than clouds, rain, the sweep
of storms and waiting.
Her feet are rooted.
Her long gaze
for the gusting trees
comes clearer than the sky. Thanks to me,

who was scarcely there
and now is gone.

Plaster of Paris

It was dark where she led me, both of us
barely thirteen, to her mother's workshop.
Rubber casts for plaster were heaped
like an orgy of emptiness. Wet clay hung
in plastic bags making heads more fearsome
than the white deer which stalked the floor.

Love at first sight. Her eyes met mine
in the Mid-America Mall. Now, uncertain first
moments, surrounded by silent
covens of the nude, powdered forest.
Ellen. I would never see her again. But we hid

behind the oven still warm and touched
as if we might feel a way to mold a life.
The Irish pointer, his body half painted,
showed the way. A nearby gnome was shy,
nodding to the open window.
Ellen's hot breath and lips were a flock
upon me. In the colorless glade, even a saint
might be swept like a pile of crumbs.
The heat grew. The dark hardened

its failed colors. Just when we would crack,
the door, her mother, the cool night
rushed in. Flurried as the geese I was flung
by my collar into the waiting
yard of birdbaths like a wide-eyed ghost.

Tossed beyond whiteness, do the dead
recall only a bleached world, a few
flushed faces? I looked back. *Again,*

her mother screamed at her.
I slunk off. A new life of shame.
Thank you, I might have said to them. I scraped
the powder from my knees and touched it
to my tongue. *Kiss off, you old bitch,* I said.
I doubt they heard me, or cared.

Swinging Bridge

Over Five Mile Creek

clatter of feet and boards,
up and down as much as forward.
Jaye keeps hold too tight
and where she stops
fear rises.

Like spit disappearing
in the clear water below
are all her hopes
of whom she'd meet,
as if two would cross at once

facing off
on planks so narrow.
She thought she'd see
that him of dreams
suddenly in the low half-way,

no rock or sway before,
no call or sign
of who's going first.
Head down, it's not her feet
but eyes that grip the boards.

If only she'd look up, see him
watching from the far bank,
she alone no longer.

Quiet Please

Hearing everything

Where everything should be silent
The ear becomes a librarian.

It reminds the young ladies and gentlemen
To be ladies and gentlemen.

Coos of love on rainy afternoons,
And at night near closing

The cough which rasps
Too harsh. It knows them all

Too well.
Like the kiss of a gnat

Is the creasing of a corner
At the page of a dark disease.

When the ear gets off work
(No one ever wants to know when)

The world must listen for itself.
Once more in the aimlessness

Of empty aisles. It seems
To go on, but does it?

The ear is silent.
Let them answer

For themselves.
In old age, the ear is hard

Of hearing. People talk behind
Its back. There's a secret joy

In this, although the work
Has never seemed so daring.

Augustine, Aquinas, the antique rarities
Beckon the ear to their covers

Of dust. *Touch me,* they say.
But the ear, too delicate now

Even for them, will not. Its skin
Grows thinner, transparent,

The blood rushing on.

Fingernails

When I was a child, Aunt Martha
was the only unmarried grown-up in the world.
She lived in distant Winter Park, where
in spite of the name, her photos said it was always
summer, blue lakes surrounded by palms,
and geese whose dangerous hard bills plucked
bread from her fingers. I'd tried it once myself
at the zoo, coming away with blood
around my nails.

A schoolteacher, unlike
the nuns at Saint Mary's she drove
a white Caddy convertible, cruising in.
Late June she lay in the terraced yard
on a thick Daytona towel, to spread
the coconut cream she said
would save her tan.

Were long, red fingernails
all that kept her from marriage?
Without children, and yet so
like my mother they were almost twins.
Once, in a rare moment of talk
I asked her why she rubbed the oil
so thick along her arms. She sipped her tea,
and raked her fingers down her arm.
Five white streaks, and the red nails filled
with skin and cream. She turned them toward me
so casually, and in terror
I ran.

The Victims of Love

One claimed
its voice was the wind,
crying around a light pole
like an animal in the vacant lot.

Another felt the warmth
escaping the sidewalk grate
as the loneliness of her body
drifting through a night of ice.

Others were uncertain.
Was the one they saw merely
remembered, a shadow
from infancy, leaning over the crib?

The line-up was no use. Each chose
a different profile, different
eyes, different way of saying
"Hand it over, and you won't get hurt."

We stare from our living room windows
while night falls on the rooftops.
Our children come to us
frightened by the windy flight of trees.

No stories will help.
The pain of kisses sweeps over us.
In a bright room together,
we try to recognize

the other beyond the mirrored glass.
Him! Her!
Love, we were so certain
we had caught you, named you,

before we forgot all you were.

Cinéma Vérité

The film maker, an old friend,
has tried to show his mother's
death from Alzheimer's
off-screen, retrieved only
by his staccato syllables breaking down,
his father's red-rimmed eyes.

In the theatre, my wife
leaning to my ear, a smooth
hush in her voice, turns me
as if to share a pleasant secret.
What if, she says,
it's all a lie?

He holds a photo of his mother
and himself, a child by the lake's edge.
He moves his thumb across,
unsteadily, unsure. The hand-
held motion. This
is memory, is real.

My wife feels the forgotten
is delicious. Easily repeated
without fear. And lies, how well
they allow us to escape.
I want to, but can't ignore
his mother's last birthday,

the film of her smiling
through the restaurant.
We carried her home struggling.
Close-ups of the family flicker past.

I am nowhere. At the end,
a still of his mother

comes to life, waving with soundless words.
She is my mother, anyone's mother,
and she is dead.
What's the truth now? My wife
cups hand to ear, leaning close.
She is my confessor and knows

I cannot tell.

Rothko

I.

I would like to tell you a story, he said.
He was sitting in his studio, you know how he was,
getting past middle age and fat, his eyes behind
those glasses growing more and more myopic.
It's about a little girl, he said,
and it has nothing to do with why you're here,
nothing to do with art I mean. It's just a story.

Emotion without image, at worst
the wonder of sitting in an empty room.

So he went on, and I was losing interest.
Half the time, you know, he didn't make sense,
like those dark paintings he did before
he died. You stare at them for hours and where
does it get you? This thing about the little girl,
it was just something about seeing her each day
on his way home, how she was always skipping rope.

II.

One rectangle is blue, another red, another yellow.
No, this sounds too simple. You can't do this
and call it a lie.

So I said, tell me what it means, and I meant
the painting he was working on, but he said
it means I hated her. He turned
and didn't say another word. Beginning to paint,

he worked the color in hard as if he were trying
to press it through the canvas.

Suicide. Approaching, its slow form
marks him like the rhyming of a poem, a color.
Shading saves the day, like love and forgiveness.

III.

The dark purple at the top is both the lid
of the grave and the spirit as it rises. Below,
the red is both the grave and the body
of the man who lies in it. Sunk into the ground,
into the burnt orange which is life,
the earth takes from the sun this empty grave.
Yes, my friend, in the field above it
which we do not see, a girl is skipping rope.
The grass is high and August turns it golden brown.
We have to imagine this.

The artist knows it is not the same for everyone.
Above the field he sees the mirror image
of the grave, a lake. The day is drifting into evening
and he can hear the girl's father calling her to dinner.
There is not enough time, enough space to get above this
    loneliness.

In the story, the girl is on a streetcorner.
The critic goes home sick
at the loss of his hero. Sentiment, he says,
where does it get you? The girl skips.
The world burns over. Burnt orange.

Mail Bomb

A coiled spring more delicate
than a child's finger, the metal
only bending one way or it will break,
and time too, moving only one way,
measured by grains falling, the tick
of a watch, the slow decay of atoms.
I am too large to understand
how quickly we are unwrapped,
the small things we are
exploded. Someone is dead,
and it's not even me.

It seems like me, my body
stunned so I realize only later
the package filled the room,
its small world of eye
becoming monstrously large,
its patient waiting for acceptance
blowing outward.
Someone will come to piece us together.
Someone will find our truth.
This is what survivors think
as they examine their hands.

The lines on their palms
appear intact, the fine hair
of their forearms unsinged,
until they see in the shattered
mirror the hundred loving faces
of as many rooms.

On Graymont Avenue

How long vacant—the coal dust
on the basement floor, the crack
in the bathroom tile that spilled
a froth of winged termites
one afternoon when I came from school?
Gone the terraced yard of iris, the fig,
all sloping in a tumble
of rocks and dirt against the back wall.

The rat's hole behind the kitchen sink
is now the size of a cat. Where my father threw
a book across the room for telling
a truth he didn't want
is the charred hole from a squatter's fire.

When we determine we will die
does life begin? One morning I woke
and went downstairs with my grandmother
and found the yellow feathers of her canary
where the rat had left them.
I had not seen her cry.

An old house, an old woman, the crying
gone out of her. In the famous Spanish story
of the nobleman in love with his queen,
not long after her death her coffin was reopened.
Her ruined face turned him
from this life to the next.

Look at the face of the house,
the windows of its sunroom are broken out,
the steps to the high front porch

are rotted through. Still, if I want
I can put them back,
fix the windows
so the sun wavers
from the hand-poured glass.
Too easy. Harder to fall in
with the rotted face. Not to fix it
but to breathe deeply.
Not going back to the queen
of my love, but forward.

Yellow Fever Cemetery

Unturned leaf, you were never very good
to begin with, like an old excuse
your gate rusted shut. The only way past
was to scramble up cracks in your stone wall,
over the iron fence along the sill, then to drop
beneath your cool, sweet cedars.
They were bigger around than we were,
spindly kids with pocket knives and cherry bombs
loose for the summer.

Go ask your dead why they're so
attractive to children when the two are left alone.
They might tell you about angels,
all of yours too young, their small, winged bodies
too precious for death. They rose over us
in carved elaborate feathers,
their faces too calm even for the wind
sighing the cedars. Patience, said the moss.
The black mildew spread across shoulders
like a wrap drawn over the fear of being slow.

Trumpets? No, we were a few wild kids
treading between slabs, peering down cracks
for the hole of a rat
to light a cherry bomb and drop it in.
Yellow fever killed the most,
dates in the eighteen-seventies,
mostly young. Two girls our age, and a boy
the same, passing in August, his anniversary

a day away. Their names were Old Testament,
Rebecca, Suzanna, Jeremiah.

Years later, to ride by the cedars
which seem no bigger now, I think of others
climbing the walls, dropping down.
Knives stab the dirt to widen a crack. We hate
ourselves. We hate you holding our dead,
to be turned over, dreamed on, forgotten,
then remembered too well.
We light the fuse and push it under, hope
for the stone slab to heave, deadly leaf,
if we're lucky, if we've done it just right.

Winter Scene

The boys are playing cards again, late night,
beers around the table. Someone throws out
a chip, another follows, the pot rises.

In the fireplace, two logs burn in the center
and a third is already ashes. An Irish setter
lies in front of the fire, asleep.

The windows are frosted. I am cold. I lie
in the bed alone. I will die alone.
It was the same for my mother.

Someone should make a movie about this,
one of the card players says. He's not
serious, just losing, and wants to be a hero.

The Irish setter dreams of a rabbit
in the deep snow, unable to run
as the long red legs bound above the drifts.

It was the same for my mother,
in bed alone, the windows frosted.
She was cold as death.

What kind of a movie? another man says.
He pictures them in suits
with tumblers of bourbon, a paddlewheel turning.

The rabbit is trapped. Until moments ago
it was asleep, not even aware
of the snow above it, and hunters moving close.

Like a frosted window, my mother,

lying in her bed alone,
cold, the same as I will be.

A movie about gamblers, the first one says.
Screw-ups like us, having a good time.
Who cares what it means?

The rabbit's heart pounds so fast
it can't breathe. The snow-dusted fur
on its back is white like its stomach.

In her bed alone, the same as I will be,
she looks to windows frosted,
but sees only the cold, my mother.

I care, one of them says. He gets up
from the table and goes to the fire.
He warms himself, pets the sleeping dog.

Illinois Poetry Series
Laurence Lieberman, Editor

Rough Cut
Thomas Swiss (1997)

Paris
Jim Barnes (1997)

The Ways We Touch
Miller Williams (1997)

The Rooster Mask
Henry Hart (1998)

The Trouble-Making Finch
Len Roberts (1998)

Grazing
Ira Sadoff (1998)

Turn Thanks
Lorna Goodison (1999)

Traveling Light: Collected and
New Poems
David Wagoner (1999)

Some Jazz a While: Collected
Poems
Miller Williams (1999)

The Iron City
John Bensko (2000)

Songlines in Michaeltree: New and
Collected Poems
Michael S. Harper (2000)

Pursuit of a Wound
Sydney Lea (2000)

The Pebble: Old and New Poems
Mairi MacInnes (2000)

National Poetry Series

Eroding Witness
Nathaniel Mackey (1985)
Selected by Michael S. Harper

Palladium
Alice Fulton (1986)
Selected by Mark Strand

Cities in Motion
Sylvia Moss (1987)
Selected by Derek Walcott

The Hand of God and a Few
Bright Flowers
William Olsen (1988)
Selected by David Wagoner

The Great Bird of Love
Paul Zimmer (1989)
Selected by William Stafford

Stubborn
Roland Flint (1990)
Selected by Dave Smith

The Surface
Laura Mullen (1991)
Selected by C. K. Williams

The Dig
Lynn Emanuel (1992)
Selected by Gerald Stern

My Alexandria
Mark Doty (1993)
Selected by Philip Levine

The High Road to Taos
Martin Edmunds (1994)
Selected by Donald Hall

Theater of Animals
Samn Stockwell (1995)
Selected by Louise Glück

The Broken World
Marcus Cafagña (1996)
Selected by Yusef Komunyakaa

Nine Skies
A. V. Christie (1997)
Selected by Sandra McPherson

Lost Wax
Heather Ramsdell (1998)
Selected by James Tate

So Often the Pitcher Goes to Water
until It Breaks
Rigoberto González (1999)
Selected by Ai

Other Poetry Volumes

Local Men and *Domains*
James Whitehead (1987)

Her Soul beneath the Bone:
Women's Poetry on Breast Cancer
Edited by Leatrice Lifshitz (1988)

Days from a Dream Almanac
Dennis Tedlock (1990)

Working Classics: Poems on
Industrial Life
*Edited by Peter Oresick and
Nicholas Coles* (1990)

Hummers, Knucklers, and Slow
Curves: Contemporary Baseball
Poems
Edited by Don Johnson (1991)

The Double Reckoning of
Christopher Columbus
Barbara Helfgott Hyett (1992)

Selected Poems
Jean Garrigue (1992)

New and Selected Poems, 1962–92
Laurence Lieberman (1993)

The Dig and *Hotel Fiesta*
Lynn Emanuel (1994)

For a Living: The Poetry of Work
*Edited by Nicholas Coles and Peter
Oresick* (1995)

The Tracks We Leave: Poems on
Endangered Wildlife of North
America
Barbara Helfgott Hyett (1996)

Peasants Wake for Fellini's
Casanova and Other Poems
*Andrea Zanzotto; edited and
translated by John P. Welle and
Ruth Feldman; drawings by
Federico Fellini and Augusto Murer*
(1997)

Moon in a Mason Jar and *What My
Father Believed*
Robert Wrigley (1997)

The Wild Card: Selected Poems,
Early and Late
*Karl Shapiro; edited by Stanley
Kunitz and David Ignatow* (1998)

Turtle, Swan and *Bethlehem in
Broad Daylight*
Mark Doty (2000)

Typeset in 10.5/13 Minion
with Gill Sans display
Designed by Dennis Roberts
Composed by Jim Proefrock
at the University of Illinois Press
Manufactured by Sheridan Books

University of Illinois Press
1325 South Oak Street
Champaign, IL 61820-6903
www.press.uillinois.edu